Table Of Contents (TOC)

Chapter 10: World Future Perspectives

Conclusion

Introduction

Money management is a crucial process for attaining financial success by managing money that includes expenses, investments, budgeting, banking and taxes.

It enables you to know where your money is going and also it helps you plan your budget wisely. It's a fundamental process that determines what you can do and what you can't.

The main ideas of money management are to help you set goals, get organized, track spending, build a budget and saving money. There are rules and tips that will help you for the rest of your life if you apply them and have them in mind.

Chapter 1: Understanding Needs

A common mistake that people make is to confuse lust and needs. Plan your needs on different scales, starting with the most important to the least important.

Make a pyramid with all of your expenses. Groceries, clothes and bills should be at the bottom of the pyramid as they are the most important in everyone's life. Then, start raising the pyramid with other less important expenses that you have. Here is an example which you should follow unless you already have one of your own:

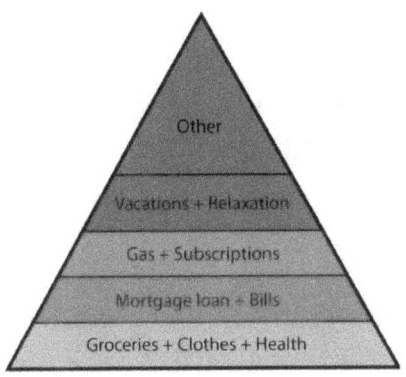

Other

Vacations + Relaxation

Gas + Subscriptions

Mortgage loan + Bills

Groceries + Clothes + Health

That should be the order of your expenses – basic needs – food, clothes and any health maintenance (drugs, gym, insurance etc.), then the mortgage loans or any other loans that you have to pay – if you dismiss this important aspect of your expenses you will get into trouble in the nearest future. Bills also have to be paid as quickly as possible. Of course, there are people who don't have to pay mortgage loans.

Next, gas (if you own a car or more), subscriptions for subways, buses or any kind of subscription that you have.

You shouldn't forget about vacations and relaxation moments – they're very important for your health and for your overall wellbeing as a person. Plan at least 1-2 vacations every year and save some money for that.

And the most interesting and expensive part is the "other" part, where most of the people don't take into consideration. If you go out for a walk and you see a new commercial for a new product, you don't think at first "do I really need this?", you just go and buy it without being rational (sometimes). This is the most common mistake of money management. This is the part which needs to be changed, tracked and managed carefully.

Every time you want to buy something you should always think:

"What would happen if I didn't buy this?"

If the answer is "nothing", then you don't actually need that to buy and you can forget about it. This is one of Warren Buffet's quotes which is very powerful for managing money.

To avoid getting into debt because of too many expenses, you need to track your money – how much you earn, how much you need and how much you spend each month and each year. To avoid getting into trouble or debt, sum up all your expenses and the sum should always be smaller than the income that you have.

Chapter 2: Living Paycheck To Paycheck

This is the most common mistake which people make all the time – you get over the month or even over the year without saving a penny. It gets even worse if you borrow money for your other expenses.

The first thing you should do is tracking your expenses, spending less money, especially on things that you don't really need.

To get rid of this habit, to live from paycheck to paycheck you should see where your money is going and to start cutting the useless subscriptions, memberships and other expenses.

When you make a subscription, let's say for your mobile phone, you must think twice – monthly and yearly. How much does it cost?

30$ / month. It doesn't sound much, but when you multiply that with 12 for the whole year, 360$ / year just for the phone bill is something.

You go even further. How much is your internet and TV subscription? 100$/ month? It's something, but in one year you pay 1200$ for it. I'm not saying to cut the internet or your TV, but find the least expensive or the best offer that you can get, if you manage to get a 60$ subscriptions you would save 480$ in one year.

Cut other things which you don't actually need – gas (if you own a car) – If you have to walk for a couple of minutes, don't take the car, it will consume a lot more than it should on the highway, you could get stuck in traffic etc. Use it only when it's necessary.

How much do you pay for food? If you go to the market without knowing exactly what to buy or what you need, you will start buying things randomly which will be eventually unused or thrown away. If you need bread, water, vegetables, spaghetti, some meat and some cereal which cost in average less than 30$, you probably go and fill your basket with all kinds of products and pay more than 50-60$. It may sound like it's nothing – 20-30$ extra money? Yes, but if you go shopping once or twice a week, you will pay extra 10-20$ each time, which is 50 – 80$ extra money each month. Transform that yearly and you will obtain another 600 – 1000$ which were uselessly spent.

If your average salary is 3000$ / month, think that you work 1-2 weeks for spending money on useless things just when you go shopping for groceries. You work half a month to cover your phone bills, internet and TV. You will probably work a few month for paying your loans, you will probably work a few weeks or months for other useless things. At the end you will be surprised to see that you work a year without saving a penny, which is a huge mistake which a lot of us make.

These are just examples which have the same conclusion – spend less, spend your money on things that you really need.

By cutting all of these useless things you can save a few thousands of dollars each year which you can save, invest or spend it on a nice vacation.

The idea is simple – when you make new subscriptions or go shopping, think how much is that per month and how much is that per year.

Chapter 3: Budget Plan

To have the best results, you need to create a well balanced budget plan and to update it every day, it won't take you more than 10 minutes.

Use Excel sheets, an agenda, a booklet or other digital tools which help you track your income and your expenses.

Even if you have a fixed income or a variable income which comes from multiple streams (online marketing, daily job, rent, dividends, bonuses etc.) spread your income into percentages:

10% - Savings (at least 10%)

50% - Mortgage, Groceries, Subscriptions, Bills

10% - Annual Savings for vacations and relaxation

10% - Invest into something or save to invest in the future

10% - Emergency Savings - you never know what could happen to you or your family, you have to save money for such unpleasant moments all the time or at least to have a sum dedicated for that (like 5000$ or so)

I have put the 10% savings first because there is a very important money management rule which says: "Pay yourself first". Now, what this rule means, is that a certain percentage of your income needs to be saved all the time – make an account in which you save the 10% (at least 10%) each month and forget about that account. You should use that account in only 2 ways:

1. Build net worth.
2. Invest

To make an automated process for this, make an automated saving to your bank – each month 10% of your income goes to that account without seeing. When you will check your account after several month or years you will be impressed how much money you have actually saved. If your salary is 3,000$ / month (net) or 36,000$ / year and you pay yourself first 10% which is 300$/ month, in one year you can save 3,600$ or in 5 years 18,000$. Sounds good, doesn't it? If you only save money occasionally, you would save a lot less money.

This rule is applied by all of the famous rich people, Warren Buffet used this rule but I think he kind of exaggerated – he paid himself first with over 70% which he invested or saved. Most of the other millionaires use this rule but they save 40-50%. It's a unique and guaranteed method for saving a lot of money, especially when you automate it and don't actually see that money (10%).

The other percentages are obvious, the basic needs and expenses which are 50% or probably more or less – it couldn't be avoided.

The 10% for vacations and relaxation should also be saved separately in an account, if you don't make any savings for this and just take money from what you barely saved the whole year, you will probably go to zero savings or worse, even getting a small loan for that (I've seen many people doing that – to borrow money for a vacation).

Investments are very important if you want to achieve financial freedom or to be more relaxed. If you save enough money to make an investment, you can also take a small amount from the "Pay yourself first" account.

Every person has during his life few emergencies – to the doctor, to the bank or for any other urgent reasons. It just happens all of a sudden. What would you do if you don't have money in that moment? Another loan?

Loans are like the devil on Earth, it literally imprisons you (through your money), so avoid making any loans or at least, as fewer as possible.

This was just an example. To be honest, I use a different method for managing my money, it probably won't fit for everybody, but for me it fits wonderfully.

30% - Pay Yourself First

20% - Investments

30% - Basic needs

10% - Vacations

10% - Emergencies

You can make your own budget plan, but just plan it as fast as possible, using your own method, your own expenses and income. Respect it, manage your money and save money.

Chapter 4: Saving Money

The best idea for money management is saving. Plan to save your money to different plans that fit you and achieve this by choosing whether to save your money on a daily, weekly or monthly basis. Use methods like the one I have presented in the previous chapter. Set percentages on your own and start saving.

You can automate weekly or monthly transfers to emergency savings, investments and retirement accounts. This will help you not to misuse the money that you earn.

Set a goal to motivate yourself towards saving more money. Increase the amount you save if you get a pay rise.

Here's a short list of simples ideas that will help you save money regularly:

1. Find out which are all the benefits of your current job – you will be surprised to find out that the company that you are working for offers for employees discounts and free memberships to different events, gym centers, product discounts similar to the ones you use at work. You can save money from buying those products or just for entertaining yourself for free.
2. Create your own items instead of buying them – there are dozens of items that you can create by yourself at home, just using a couple of tools. For example, if your chair or tablet just broke and you need one to put it outside in your garden, don't just go to buy a new one (which is probably made out of plastic), find some pieces of wood and craft one of your own. Find out what items you need and create ones of your own (if it's possible).
3. Ask for any kind of fees that may appear – whenever you see a new

service, a new membership, a new bank or any kind of service, don't forget to ask for fees – this will significantly reduce your monthly bills.

4. Cancel the cable channels that you don't watch anymore – a TV channel package has a lot of channels that people don't actually watch – you probably watch a couple of channels of documentaries, music and probably a one for news. More than 50% are useless and you pay for them. Cut the ones that you don't watch and reduce your bill by up to 50%.

5. Pay your bills online – you will save time and money (commissions) – it's a lot faster and it's also comfortable.

6. Switch your bank account to the best bank you can find – choose the bank which is the most respectable and has the lowest fees. You can save a few hundreds of dollars each

year by cutting of the greedy commissions of banks.

7. Use the 30-day rule – think about an item that you want to buy. Wait for at least 30 days and check if you still want that item. If you don't want it anymore, it means that you don't really need it and it would've been a useless purchase.

8. Use the 10-second rule – before putting an item into your basket or before paying for it, wait and focus for 10 seconds – ask yourself if you really need it and what would happen if you didn't buy it. If the answer is "nothing", it means that you don't need it and you should put the item back on the shelf.

9. Before going to a grocery store, write down a list of what you need – when you will arrive at the grocery store you will know exactly what you need to buy without taking other unnecessary products.

10.   Don't throw old items, repair them – a lot of people have in their

houses items and even clothes which they don't use anymore. Most of them throw them out without thinking a second that they are actually throwing their money. In some cases, giving old items and clothes to poor people is considered a positive action and it's advisable to do so, but if you take the items to throw them to the trash can, think twice before doing that.

11. Give up smoking and excessive drinking – this is better for both your health and your financial status. In New York, a pack of cigarettes costs nearly 15$ and in the rest of the US, it costs between 5 and 10$. If you smoke 1 pack/day and a pack costs 10$, in 30 days you pay 300$ and in 1 year you pay 3,600$ just for smoking – for that money you can buy a second hand car, renew your home or go on vacation for almost a month. Drinking is also very

expensive, especially if you are used to drinking every day or every week. Try to drink only occasionally.

12. Prepare your food at home – don't eat at restaurants all the time and try to make your own food – it's a lot healthier and economical.

13. Before you buy a car, make a short list of what you can afford and which car has the lowest fuel consumption and the lowest maintenance costs. You can save 50-100$ each month by making a right choice.

14. Avoid shopping centers for entertainment – if you have nothing to do, don't go to malls just to see what's new – you will be tented to buy something, even if you don't need to.

15. Rent your home – if you are living in a big house, rent the unused space – if you pick a fair rental price, you can live for free in your own home. If your home has

1,000 square meters and you live into 500, rent the other half for a fair price depending on the region that you live in.

16.   Start your own garden – it's very easy, entertaining, low cost and benefic for you – you can plant some vegetables and eat from your own garden, all you need is some seeds and time to water them.

17.   Turn off the lights before leaving your home – if you leave the lights on when you leave your home, not only that you waste energy and you increase your electricity bill, but you might even increase the change of igniting your own home.

18.   Take food with you on road trips – don't stop over for a bite – you will waste precious money – make some sandwiches home, it's cheap and fast.

19.   Plan for cheap vacations – instead of going on an expensive

vacation each year, plan for a more cheap vacations.

20.   Don't give up on yourself whatever you do. There is always a chance to win.

Chapter 5: Investing

It's very important to save money to invest, not to save just to keep it in a bank account. It's about how much you invest and how much you get back in return. This is what investing is all about.

It's a lot more important to increase your total income rather than saving a bigger amount of money – if you save 100,000$, but your income is still 2,500$/month, you won't be able to do too many things because in case you spend money from your savings account (from the 100,000$ sum), you will lose almost everything – you haven't done anything with that money.

With that 100,000$ if you manage to save it (for example) you can buy a cheap real estate property or at least get a loan to buy a more expensive one – rent it out and make sure that you get enough rent to cover the monthly payment and you also get a small profit – in time you will get a lot of profit and the property will remain yours. After some years you can resell it or just continue renting it. It won't make you too rich, but you will manage to generate an additional amount of money every time.

This is just an example, you can invest into stocks, mutual funds, a retirement program or into other profitable niches that you may find.

The essential idea here is to invest the money that you save, not to keep all your money in a bank account.

Chapter 6: Setting Goals

Goals allow you to achieve what you desire in your future. Be flexible and determine how much you can afford to save each month for your goals. You can also set cheaper goals that are similar to the goal you had set and this will help you manage your money effectively.

If you want to increase your income and manage your money better, the first thing you want to do is to set some goals.

Goals have to be set on a weekly, monthly and yearly basis – for example, your weekly goal is to save 100$, your monthly goal at least 400$ and in 1 year you set a goal to save at least 5,000$. In a few years, you can invest some money into small businesses as I have mentioned earlier, find the ones that fit you best, which have the lowest risks and the best return on investment (ROI).

You can set not only financial goals, but productivity goals and personal goals. This helps you develop yourself on a lot of personal areas including the financial one.

If you don't have any goals, you don't have any motivation, so you it will be more likely to spend money uselessly and to give up.

You don't want that.

Make sure to respect and achieve the goals that you set for yourself, otherwise you have just wasted your time.

Chapter 7: Prioritize Debt Payments

If you want to manage your money properly, you should list all the debts that you have and list from the smallest to the largest ones.

Pay off the debt that charges the highest rates first and rearrange all of them. Consider the terms of any of your agreement so that you don't violate and get penalties. Pay minimum on credit cards and monthly required payments on loans. This will help you to pay off your debts on time and save you from any other debt trouble.

In other words, you need to create a debt management plan to reduce the costs and total amount of payments to save as much money as possible.

If you feel you can't do this by yourself, there are several small companies which study your debts, interests that you pay and they convert all of those small payments that you have into just one. This will help you know how much you have to pay every month and will help you avoid in getting into trouble.

Also contact all of your loaners and ask for smaller interests or for payment reschedules – it won't cost you a penny to ask.

Seek for any advantage that you can from all of these loaners and pay the ones which are the most important first.

The most important advice that I can give you is to STOP borrowing money – try to use the financial resources that you have, don't borrow uselessly. In my opinion, the only 2 reasons for which I would borrow money are for starting a serious business which I know 100% that it will eventually work or for buying a house if I don't have enough money to buy one. All of the other loans are useless and painful in time. Avoid them as much as possible. You will never be financially free unless you stop borrowing money.

Chapter 8: Emotional vs. Rational Decisions

Money management is highly influenced by the decisions that we make. Some of the decisions that we make can be advantageous while others may result to failure.

Emotional decisions and rational decisions are the main ways that we can approach problem solving in money management.

Rational decisions involve a systematic selection of possible choices based on reasons and facts. It's a formal process where the decision maker has full information about alternatives and has the choices that will maximize his benefits.

Emotional decisions are the decisions that are impacted by the physiological signals and they are the ring that connects reason with action. The emotional decisions can be either anticipated (immediate emotions) and they greatly affect the decisions that we make on money management. Regardless of either positive or negative emotions, they contribute on how we manage money.

Thus decisions can be addressed emotionally hence making more complex decisions rationally. Some activities lead to immediate dangers and as a result money has to be spent in curbing the danger.

In such case emotional decisions are significant in determining the best solution.

Emotional decisions help to determine the final decisions that can influence money management. When managing money the emotional decisions drive us in directions conflicting with self-interest.

Time influences how we manage money and our emotions too.

Emotional decisions tend to consider these time delays as the decision is being contemplated. This makes the individual involve hyperbolic discounting and affective discounting when managing money.

Intense emotions tend to negate the probability of the possible outcome of money management. When the individual has positive emotional decisions he/she can be motivated to make decisions inhibiting money management. Emotional decisions can also result to various cons in managing money. It can lead to poor emotional quick decisions that may lead to misuse of money rather than saving.

The immediate and unrelated emotions can create mistakes by distorting and creating bias in money management. This leads to unexpected and reckless actions that will result to poor money management.

When an individual has negative emotions he/she can spend the money on unintended things thus distorting the mechanism of managing money properly.

Anger may lead to poor emotional decisions hence causing havoc in money management. Some complex issues cannot be solved by emotional decisions and if the individual uses the emotions to make the final conclusion it can lead to failure and money will be mismanaged.

Rational decisions affect money management in many ways. When managing money using the rational decision mechanism you have to: define the problem, identify criteria, allocate weights to the criteria, develop the alternatives, evaluate the alternatives and finally, selecting the best alternative.

These are the main multi-steps in rational decision making. It influences money management and it requires discipline, consistency and logic. It is the best way to manage money since the individual will choose the best solution.

Some actions can lead to misuse of money and thus rational decisions help to choose the right action to take. There are minimal cases of errors since the individual has a wide range of measurable criteria and it can be collected easily.

Before an individual finds the best money management techniques, he/she can have cognitive abilities, time and resources to evaluate each alternative against the other one.

Rational decisions leave out consideration of personal feelings, loyalties, or sense of obligation. Its objectivity creates a bias towards the preference of facts and analysis over desires thus influencing money management negatively. The rational decisions help in maximizing benefits and making money, employing logic, achieving objectives of money management and minimizing costs thus saving more money.

Both the rational and emotional decisions have to be considered before taking the final action.

This can help in managing money appropriately and effectively without spending an extra penny. The decisions are dependent on one another. This means that for you to make alternatives via rational decisions you have to consider the emotions to be set. The vice versa is true. To make emotional decisions you have to consider various alternatives before jumping to conclusion.

Chapter 9: Seek for support

Family is one of the pillars in money management. If you have a family, arrange a system that they will incorporate for handling money and ensure that they are involved and they understand it.

Family can help you decide on the best mechanisms/systems that you can use to save your money.

Family can help you pay your loans or any other debt trouble that you got into. We live in an expensive world, so your family has to understand today's needs for existence.

Alternatively, you can seek help from institutions that will give you advice for money management. There are online websites that can also help you in managing your money.

Chapter 10: World Future Perspectives

It's very important to take into consideration how the world around you evolves. To achieve your future financial goals it's very important to speculate any ways to generate money.

Keep yourself up to date with everything, it will have big advantages in front of anybody else.

Let me give you an example – real estate properties tend to change their price all the time, if you want to obtain a long term profit, you can follow when is the lowest price point (where you should buy a property) and where is the highest price point (where you should sell it and get your profit).

There are things which you should consider or which you should be aware about.

For example – The price of education has increased with almost 1000% in the past 25 years. In a lot of prestigious universities in the United States, it can cost from 40,000$ up to 150,000$ a year. If you have to go the university for 4 years, you have to pay from 200,000$ to 600,000$. That's an insane amount of money. Few people afford to pay that price for education and not everybody who pays this price will succeed in the future.

What I am pointing at is that now you have the possibility to learn anything you want or you need from online platform such as Udemy, YouTube or recognized online platforms. You can pay 250 – 1,000$ for a professional course, you can go to some training seminars, attend to webinars and you can become yourself a professional and you can get started making money.

What you should understand from this is that you can make money from online courses, platforms etc. which weren't widely known few years ago.

Being aware of this you can create a new income stream which will help you manage your money better.

This is just a simple example, the whole idea here is to SPECULATE anything that you see profitable and be aware that the world is changing every day as you read this.

Actually, a lot of millionaires became millionaires thanks to speculations. They had some money, they bought actions, stocks, properties and in several years they obtained insane profits.

Let's talk about Amazon. If you bought Amazon stocks back in 1997 for example, being aware of the expansion of the internet (it was quite predictable to be that way) – you could've bought 5,000 market shares (stocks) with 2$/stock and just now you would've got 380$/stock which is 190 times more than you invested. You would've got a total profit of 1,900,000$ or in other words, you would've become a millionaire.

It's true that you don't know for sure what will happen, but sometimes you have to take some risks.

If you risk you may win or you may lose, but if you don't risk, you have already lost from the very first beginning.

What I am trying to tell you, be aware of everything that surrounds you, you will never know when you have the opportunity to achieve financial freedom, luck comes without giving you a sign, it just comes.

Conclusion

Managing money is essential if you want to succeed in life and if you want to accomplish your dreams. It doesn't matter how much money you have, if you don't manage it properly, you will eventually waste it all without realizing.

I hope you have understood the importance of managing money and I hope that the methods and the examples from this book will be useful to you in the future.

Thank you,

John